Y0-AAF-422

And So Man Dreams

Bruce Kaduk

Morning Star Books
P.O. Box 1354
Morristown, New Jersey 07962

Copyright 1991 by Bruce Kaduk

All rights reserved. No part of this publication may be reproduced
or transmitted in any manner whatsoever without written permission
from the publisher except in the case of brief quotations in reviews.
All inquiries should be addressed to Morning Star Books,
P.O. Box 1354, Morristown, New Jersey 07962.

Second Printing

PUBLISHED BY MORNING STAR BOOKS
Morristown, New Jersey 07962

Library of Congress Catalog Card No.: 89-090992
ISBN 0-9621914-1-8

Printed in the United States of America

For Cecilia

Without a dream
    there is no hope.
And so man dreams.
Man dreams
    when he is asleep
    and dreams
    when he is awake.
The dream is a flight,
    a flight away from
    a reality that is
    often harsh and
    always inexplicable.
The dream is a submersion,
    a submersion into
    a soul that is
    often entangled and
    always mysterious.
Without a dream
    there is no hope.
And so man dreams.

Whatever man has ever
made with his hands or
envisioned with his mind or
hoped for with his spirit
has been created
out of some combination of
earthly passion and
divine intelligence.

Look up at the sky
on a clear evening
and contemplate the scene—
    stars
    moon
    beams of light
    heavenly bodies.
It is part of a vast
and profound universe.
Look deep within your soul
on a quiet and calm evening
and contemplate the scene—
    memories
    longings
    desires
    fears.
It is part of a vast
and profound universe.

What is it—
> the fear of loneliness
> the demands of a livelihood
> the terror of being different
> the burdens of everyday life
> the loss of childhood wonder
> the lack of contact with our inner selves

What is it—
> that makes us
> a fraction of what
> we could be?

The earth will never relinquish
its hold on you.
Through its gravity,
the earth always and at all times
attracts you to its core.
But the earth has no hold on your spirit.
Gravity exerts no force on the human spirit.
Let that spirit
be your release and
your escape
from the earth's
incessant and stubborn hold.

That which makes us happy
as human beings
has
    a different form
    a different texture
    a different composition
than that which makes us
    prominent or
    powerful or
    renowned.

Human perfection resides not in the reality,
    but in the imagination.
Human perfection resides
    not in the action
        but in the action imagined
    not in the response
        but in the response imagined
    not in the pleasure
        but in the pleasure imagined
    not in the fulfillment
        but in the fulfillment imagined.

The most profound challenge
in thinking for oneself
is not the intellectual,
    but the social challenge.
If one is to think
for himself,
he must do it
    alone.

Stamped indelibly
on our psyches
is the instinct
to be concerned
with our own needs.
This self-concern
        is what preserves us.
The transcendence of this self-concern
        is what exalts us.

The human species is you and
it is me,
it is every person who has ever lived
        and every person who ever will live,
it is instinct and impulse,
it is blind force and awesome energy,
it is intellect and passion, and
it is, taken in its entirety,
        absolutely beyond comprehension.

In the earliest preferences
of the child
lie the inclinations
of the adult.

Always
	propagating
	generating
	flowering
	yielding
	bringing forth—
why is it
that nature
overflows with
inexhaustible
creativity?

In dreams
In idle thoughts and feelings
In wishes and yearnings—
    there are clues
    to the secrets
    of our inner worlds.

Life is
    the excursion
    the voyage
    the journey
    the adventure.
Death is
    the return home.

We speak of virtue as if we know,
for certain, what virtue is.
We speak of virtue as if it is
some ideal conduct of life
that is in opposition
to our inherent nature.
Maybe virtue is precisely the opposite.
Maybe virtue is that conduct of life
that is precisely in accord with
        the particular dreams
        the particular talents
        the particular strengths
        the particular nature
of each of us.
Maybe virtue is nothing but
        the affirmation
        of life.

Everything
that is new
is born of
turmoil and
turbulence.

Listen closely
to the music
of Bach and Beethoven.
Listen closely and attentively
because there
you will find revealed,
sometimes subtly and
sometimes dramatically,
 the variations
 the contours
 the transformations
 the complexities
of basic human emotion.

An eternity of time
existed before we were born.
An eternity of time
will exist after we die.
Our death will only return us
to a place
we have already been.

Not until we recognize
the creature
within us
can we understand
the universe
outside us.

Because man is mortal,
because the physical is in conflict
    with the spiritual,
because the conscious is in conflict
    with the unconscious,
because the intellectual is in conflict
    with the instinctual,
because of this—
    human life pulsates with
    passion and
    intensity and
    turmoil.

Only because
we are uninvolved observers
does the life of another
look better
than our own.

Every time love arises,
every time the electricity of passion flows,
every time the flame of desire burns in the soul—
       what you are witnessing is
       the absolutely natural inclination
       of the human species
       to endure.

Played by a master,
the strings of a violin
vibrate
to the frequencies
of the human soul.

Different religions
different beliefs
different songs
different prayers—
Don't they exist
to deal with
the same fears
the same confusions
the same questions
the same perplexities?

The real miracle is
that we are here
that we are conscious
that we are alive.

To remain human,
to remain in touch with
        your feelings and instincts,
to remain conscious of the
        ever changing soul within you—
is to fight,
every day of your life,
against the innumerable forces
around you
that would have you
do otherwise.

Love
    ennobles and
    exalts and
    liberates
because
love enters
    the most sacred realms of
the individual soul
the human soul
the universal soul.

We are a part of nature.
We are born and we die
        according to nature's design.
We live our brief lives in a universe
        that runs solely according to nature's laws.
Small wonder, then, that our real happiness
        cannot be derived from human inventions.
Small wonder, then, that man's real happiness,
        in every age of history,
        has come from
        the very same source.

Let us rejoice
    in the body and
    in the mind and
    in the imagination and
    in the dream and
    in the feeling and
    in the thought
because they
have been given
to us and
because they
are ours.

That which is brought to the surface
from the depths of the unconscious mind,
that which is brought to a state
of awareness and consciousness—
    can no longer
    rule us.

There is
a death
 of the spirit and
 of the soul
that is a
different kind of death
than the death of the body
and it is
 this living death
 this death in life
that we must fight
and fight with everything
we have
because it is
by far
the worst kind
of death
there is.

The secrets of nature
are revealed
nowhere more clearly
than in
the mechanism of your own being
the workings of your own consciousness
the yearnings of your own heart.

It is not only true
that life is a struggle—
it is also true
that this struggle,
more than anything else,
can give life
     energy and
     depth and
     purpose.

Our longing for love,
our unending longing for love
is,
more than anything else,
a longing
        for release and
        for freedom
from
the intrinsic boundaries
of human existence.

The universe was not made
for man.
The universe existed
before man existed.
Even if man
did not exist,
the universe
would still exist,
would still be infinite,
would still be incomprehensible,
would still be inexplicable
          and profound.

Amid
the noise and clamor
the chaos and confusion
the uproar and tumult
the struggle and conflict—
　　it is a miracle
　　that the voice
　　of the individual
　　human soul
　　can be heard
　　at all.

Nothing is as expansive
as the understanding of one's own self
because it leads
to an understanding of other selves
and
to an understanding of the
    intricacies and
    mysteries and
    labyrinths
of every self
that exists.

Human life is but one
of a million varieties of life
that radiate
from every corner and
from every depth and
from every surface
of the earth.

The soul withers if we do not tend to it.
The soul dies under the weight of
    too much wanting
    too much fear.
The soul is a temporary possession.
It is ours for a brief moment in time.
It is nourished by
    freedom
    beauty
    affection
    awareness
    courage.
The soul withers if we do not tend to it.
The soul dies
    without even a sound.

Consciously or unconsciously,
every man knows
that beauty is eternal.
Before the majesty
of nature
we are quiet
for a reason.

There is
more magic
        in the rhythm of human emotions
        in the colors of human imagination
        in the transformations of the human soul
than there is
in the yearnings
of human beings
        for prestige
        for position
        for power.

When passion is suppressed and
when feeling is subdued
so that reason can prevail and
intellect can triumph,
is not something lost
for that which is gained?

Courage on the battlefield
        is one kind of courage.
But it is not
        the only kind.
And, probably, it is not
        the most important kind.
There is the courage of the mind
        to think independent thoughts and
        to form independent judgments.
There is the courage of the heart
        to believe in and
        to trust one's own feelings and instincts.
There is the courage of the spirit
        to value and
        to celebrate life
        in spite of
        every difficulty and
        every obstacle.

Human desire
is not peripheral.
It is central.
It is at the core
    of living
    and
    of life
    itself.

Are we not instinct
       as much as knowledge?
Are we not impulse
       as much as thought?
Are we not sensuality
       as much as spirituality?
Are we not body
       as much as soul?

The mystery of love
is equalled only
by the mystery
of that place
in the human soul
that love reaches.

What is the cause
where is the location
who is the originator
of that something
in the human psyche
that makes us
profoundly conscious,
not of what
        we have,
but of what
        we have not?

Faith and fact are not incompatible.
The universe does exist.
Man does exist.
The facts, alone, are astounding.
The facts, alone, are grounds
        for faith.

We must remain human.
We must resist that which makes life
    mechanical
    unfeeling
    automatic
    indifferent
    unresponsive.
We must encourage that which makes life
    intimate
    imaginative
    colorful
    creative
    joyful.
We must remain human.

Man
is
matter given form
substance given order
idea given reality.

Why do we look to supernatural events
for revelation of the miraculous?
Are not nature
and life
miracle enough?

Something in man
    is immortal.
Something in man
    lives on.
Something in the far reaches
    of the soul,
something tough and invincible
    will never be destroyed
    will never be extinguished
by an event
as common and ordinary
as death.

What is remarkable
        is not that
        a man's life should end.
What is remarkable
        is that
        it should have begun.

About the Author

Bruce Kaduk was born in Easton, Pennsylvania. He is author of two other collections of philosophical poetry – *Illuminations* and *Of Human Freedom.*

He was educated at Franklin and Marshall College and later at Rutgers University where he received a Ph.D. in chemistry. He spent his career as an industrial polymer chemist and lives with his wife in New Jersey.